LinkedIn Secrets

inDEX

Why LinkedIn?

As of today when I am writing this book, LinkedIn has over 1 Billion Users.

The HRs, the Managers, the Founders, the CEOs, the CXOs, the CFOs, the Influencers,

Everyone is Present on LinkedIN

Whether you are looking for a Job or want to crack a client for your services, you know what I mean to say?

The People who can get you this, are on LinkedIN.

2 million posts, articles and videos are Published on LinkedIn every day. 3 Million users post on LinkedIn every week. On an Average, user spends 7.27 minutes on LinkedIn per visit.

And this is the answer to "Why LinkedIN?"

LinkedIn Myths

1. I need a lot of followers for getting client attention.
   Yeah, it's a myth. It's busted in the book further.

2. People don't reply to the messages.
   This is the myth and belief of so many people & It'll also
   be busted in the Book Further.

About the Author

Hi, I am Varun Midge, a 20 Year Old, third year Electrical Engineering Student at Walchand College of Engineering, Sangli. I am from Pune basically.

I am a Founder of "PixonX" which is an Agency where I provide services like LinkedIn Lead Generation & AI Based Video Content Creation to Businesses.

I have also started ONE STEP AT A TIME Podcast on my YouTube Channel. The Podcast for 20 Year Olds who want to make it big in their lives. I create content on Instagram as well.

You might think, how will a 20 year old guy tell me how I can get Clients from LinkedIn or Expand my Business.

I would think the same way, but the reason is, I have spent more time on LinkedIn than most people would have.

Make sure you click a photo of this book, and tag me on the Socials.

LinkedIn: Varun Midge
Instagram: @varunmidge820
Twitter(X.com): @varyms
YouTube: www.youtube.com/@varunmidge2884

Special THANKS to my Parents Mangesh Midge(Dad), Seema Midge(Mom), Mandar Midge(Uncle) for motivating me, for supporting me in whatever I am doing, in whatever I am hustling and for helping me stay grounded and Grow..!

Thanks to my Mentors Raj Gupta, Sachin, Prity Kar, Bharat, for encouraging me. I have been learning a lot from these folks.

Without all these Amazing People, this book wouldn't have been released!!!

To the Reader:
Thanks for taking out your time and attention to Read this Book. I have tried my best to put whatever knowledge I have about LinkedIn into this Book!! You've taken the decision to learn and grow yourself. You are different from most of the people out there who are busy finding their gfs and bfs or chilling on Netflix.

Now, let's dive right in!!

Introduction

I won't be describing here what LinkedIn is. Because, if you all are here, you already know about it. It's that easy.
According to me, LinkedIn is the only Platform right now which can open you to the opportunities you can't even think of.

I came across LinkedIn while I was preparing for IITJEE.

Hi, I am Varun Midge, a 20 Year Old, third year Electrical Engineering Student at Walchand College of Engineering, Sangli. My HomeTown is Pune.

I am a Founder of "PixonX" which is an Agency where I provide services like LinkedIn Lead Generation & AI Based Video Content Creation to Businesses.

I started my journey when I was in my 8th Grade when I got access to the Internet and a Laptop. The Financial Condition of my Family was not well and that's why I always had an urge to do something online and make money. Hence, I always used to watch Online Money Making videos on youtube. Also, I used to follow Aman Dhattarwal, Vivek Bindra. But, nothing was getting figured out during that time.

I scored 94.60% in my 10th Boards. My family was very happy and suggested that I take Science Stream and so did I.

Also in Covid, I learnt about Graphic Design, Social Media Marketing, Content and stuff. Applied for various Contributor Programs on various platforms. Also applied for various Internships. Got one unpaid Internship, I lived it in 15 days as I was unable to manage my studies with it.

I was preparing for IIT-JEE MAINS and JEE ADVANCED Exams, but I failed in both. I scored just 74.67% in my 12th Boards. I also appeared for MHT-CET(State Level Engineering Entrance of Maharashtra State). I scored 95%ile in it which got me into Walchand College of Engineering in Sangli, a town 200 kilometers away from my Home Town - Pune.

When I got into college, I again started researching ways to make money online. And I suddenly discovered that I have got selected for one of the Contributor Programs which I applied to before during the Covid Time. This Blew my Mind and I started working on that. It grew slowly and steadily. And this was my first Income Source. My first income was 3000 Rupees which was accumulated in a whole year. Then this thing kept growing and then it became constant.

After some days, when I reached the 2nd year of my Engineering, I came across two folks on Instagram, Joy Anand and Sahil Kasana. They had a free program, where they would shortlist young hustling people and help them grow. -

I got selected into that. I had a few mentorship meetings with Sahil. They made me aware of the Agency Business. I realised the potential of LinkedIn due to them. I am very Grateful to them for opening my Mind.

After that, I started creating content on Instagram and I thought let's create content on LinkedIn as well. So, I started optimizing my LinkedIn. I started posting about whenever I went to any interesting events, or my learnings. But, I was not so consistent but this thing kept going....

Also, I used to try a lot of stuff with my Childhood Friend Kunal. I started YouTube Thumbnail and YouTube Video Editing Business with my Friend Kunal, but it didn't work out.

Then I started a Dental Marketing Agency ORASPEC with my Friend Yash and I tried to get clients for it from LinkedIn, but LinkedIn didn't work out for me at that time. Till then, I had started believing that LinkedIn doesn't work..! We spent around 9 months on Building ORASPEC. I tried Cold Calling to get Indian Dentists as Clients. We did many Sales Calls but ended up converting 0. I was almost depressed at that time. But, every comeback has a breakthrough!

Then recently in October 2024, I came across Raj Gupta's Ads on Instagram. I attended his Webinar. I also bought his course and he unveiled the real power of LinkedIn to me.

And since then, I have been mind-tuned. I never knew it had such a huge Potential. He opened my Mind to the things which I haven't explored yet.

I started reaching out to the People with the Framework which Raj taught us.! I understood the game of what makes people reply back.

And you won't believe it, but I started getting replies from Founders, Investors. I booked appointments and hopped on the sales calls and started pitching for my Services of Lead Generation & AI Based Video Content Creation.

Also, I was always curious to know how successful people make it big in their lives or reach at big levels, the People who are Influencers and have lakhs and thousands of followers, the people who are Investors, the startup owners.

I always had a dream of starting my own Podcast. So, I thought let's give it a try through LinkedIn. So I started approaching the Founders, Tech Startup Owners, HNIs, VCs, Influencers for the Podcast. And believe it or not, but I got some of these People on my Podcast. As of now, there is only 1 Podcast live on my Channel. But there are 3 Podcasts in Pipeline which will be released till the end of Feb.

In the Following Chapters, we will go deep into how your profile must look like, how you can get a job, crack a deal and everything about it…!

LinkedIn Profile

When it comes to Linkedin or any Platform. The first and most important thing is "Profile". Our Profile must be appealing so that the people must like to explore it.

Profile Photo:
- Your Profile photo must be decent, shot in a good lit environment, and professional.
- Ensure your face is clearly visible, with a front-facing, high-definition image.
- Use a neutral or non-distracting background.

You can view the Profile Photos of these folks: Raj Gupta, Prity Kar, Ishan Sharma, and mine too. Feel free to hire a Photographer if you can to get the best Profile Picture.

LinkedIn Profile Banner:
- Your banner should be visually appealing and resonate with what you do, whom you help and how you help.
- You can also include your achievements here, for eg. you are a bestselling author, you gave a Ted Talk, you own a Podcast etc.
- Utilize design tools like Canva for templates or pfpmaker.com for creating professional backgrounds.

You can view the Banners of these folks: Raj Gupta, Prity Kar, Ishan Sharma, and mine too.

LinkedIn Bio:

Your Bio must include what you do, whom you help, how you help, your achievements, it's a bit similar to banners.
You can add your services, you're a founder, what you are building currently, your USP, etc.

For Example:
My Bio:

Varun Midge ✅ (He/Him)

Helping Businesses & Coaches to Scale by Converting Connections into Customers | High-Ticket Leads & Sales Strategist | LinkedIn Sales Expert | Get your Calendar booked | Host: OSAT Podcast | Founder: PixonX

Another Examples:

Raj Gupta (Lead Generation) ✅ · 1st

Growth Marketing | Helping Coaches & Marketers With High Ticket Leads and Sales | LinkedIn Sales Machine Strategist | B2B Lead Generation | Generated 200K$ in Revenue in 2024

Ishan Sharma (He/Him) · 2nd

Building Sentora & MarkitUp | YouTuber with 1M+ subs | BITS Goa | Helping Brands Grow on YouTube

This is what most people use "|" to separate different things in a bio.
Your Bio should not be like this:
Student at Walchand College of Engineering, Sangli
or
WCE Electrical'26

So many college students do this.

Student at XYZ College or University.

But this is totally ineffective and won't work at all.

For Example: Whenever someone is searching for a "Video Editor", he or she would click on a Profile which is mentioning Video Editing in a Bio and not the name of the College.

A Pro Tip: Think about what you are doing differently than others and mention that thing also in your Bio.

About Section:
The section gives you full freedom to express your thoughts about yourself, what you do, whom you help, how you help people, your qualities and what not.

You can write your ABOUT in 2700 characters.

You should use Bullet Points here to express things rather than using Big Paragraphs. People tend to consume or read short things.

Try to involve as many keywords as you can about your Niche or Industry.

Many People also write their full story in the About Section and that is good, people like to read and listen to stories.

Contact Info:

Here, you give your contact info such as Mobile Number, Email ID, your website(if you have). So that the people can easily get in touch with you.

Featured Section:

Here, you can feature your best posts on LinkedIn, also you can showcase your YouTube Channel or Instagram account here. You can add 5 objects here. If you add more, they go into see more.

Education Section:

Here, you can put your Education Details. Your College or University you graduated from, the year you have graduated in or will graduate in, your stream.

You can also mention your 12th and 10th Grade School, Marks or Grade

Licenses & Certification:

Here you can showcase the Certifications you have earned from the online or offline courses or workshops you did, everything about it. That can be even from websites like Udemy or Coursera.

You can link your certificates here so that people can view the certificate by just clicking on it.

Skills:

Here, you can add all the Skills you have, the Practical Skills, your knowledge, everything.

Endorsements:

Here, the people who have worked with you can come and Endorse you for those skills. They have an option to tell LinkedIn about if they worked with you on a Project, or heard about you from someone else, etc.

Accomplishments:

It has following things:

- **Courses**

  You Can add here the list of Courses you did.

- **Honors & Awards**

  The awards, scholarships, hackathons you've won.

- **Languages**

  The Languages you can speak

- **Projects**

  Here, you can showcase what projects you've worked on. You can mention everything about the technology you used, the tools you used for the Project.

- **Publications**

  Here you can mention about the Blogs you were mentioned in, or articles you were mentioned in.

- **Patent**

  This section is for Researchers and Professors who have filed Patents or have made Research Papers.

- **Organization**

  If you have worked for an NGOs or NPOs. You can describe here exactly what you did. Ex. You taught Mathematics to Kids for 1 month.

LinkedIn Connections

Whenever you discover a person on LinkedIn, you can connect and follow him/her.

You can directly follow them.

But for connecting, you have two options, sending just a connection request, and sending a personalized invite.
Now, here is the real game.

The person's probability of accepting the connection request is more when you send a personalized invite..!

Hence, you must always send a personalized invite..! Now, you can send many connection requests but you can send only 5 Personalised connections in a month. Yes, only five. If you want to send more, you need to get LinkedIn Premium.

But don't worry, that's not an issue. You can get LinkedIn Premium for a very low price by referrals. You can get it easily.

After you get LinkedIn Premium, don't send more than 30 connection requests per day. Or LinkedIn may consider you as a spammer and may BAN your Account, or terminate your account temporarily.

And all set!!

Now, I want an oath from you that you'll send at least 20 connection requests everyday to your target audience or your prospects.

Now, let's understand how connections really work. For you, connections are divided into 4 levels, 1st degree, 2nd degree, 3rd degree, 3+ Connection.

The 1st Degree connections are the people you have already connected with.

The 2nd Degree connections are the people who are connected with your 1st degree connections.

The 3rd Degree connections are the people who are connected with your 2nd degree connections.

The people in 3+ Degree are generally people who don't have any connection with your connections or your industry.

Now, who is our target audience?

Our target audience are the people in our 2nd degree connections.

Understanding the Customer

People of mostly all Professions are Active on LinkedIn. Now, you must understand thoroughly and properly, your Target Audience.

The People who are your Customers, the People who can help you with Jobs in case you're looking for a Job through LinkedIn.

For Example:
If you are an "App Developer". i.e. You help People with Developing an App.

Then, your Target Audience is:
- Online Ecommerce Businesses
- Serial Entrepreneurs who might be looking to develop an app for their next venture.
- Tech Investors, because they have contacts in the Industry, and they can connect you with the People who might need an App to be Developed.

So, these people must be Mentioning these things in their Profile.

So you can reach out to these People. How? It's in the next Chapter

This was for Outreaching stuff.

Now, if we talk about Content, then, you can't grow your audience if you're targeting a very small niche. You have to target a broad audience. And make content which would resonate with that broad audience.

For Example:
I met a Person from the US who runs a Website where he makes it easier for founders to hire Talented Students from Harward, etc universities at minimal cents an hour.

So, he makes content around freelancing tips, etc to attract the student Audience.

Finding your Customers

On LinkedIn, there is a search bar, where you can find People, Posts, Job Postings, Events, and a lot of stuff.

Now, to find your Customer. Think, what your customer must have been mentioning in his/her Bio, About, Posts, Experience, etc.

For Example:
You are a Video Editor, then as we discussed in the above Chapter, Understanding the Audience, your Ideal Prospect/Customer must be mentioning "Content Creator", "Youtuber", etc in their Profile.

So, to find those, what you have to do is, search the keyword Content Creator in double quotes in the Search Bar and set the filter to People.

For Example:
Search *"Content Creator"*
And it will filter out all the People who have *"Content Creator"* mentioned in their Profile
And you are good to go. Cheers!

Also, you can find your Customers in the
- Likes & Comment section of the Posts of the Top Personality(Influencer) in your Niche.
- Events on Linkedin. There are attendees listed.

LinkedIn Messaging

This is crucial!!
This is a part of Sales too.
You can get a Job Referral through People!
You can get a client!

You cannot get a person to reply by sending anything like
All of these just through a proper message.

Hey Varun,
I am Ravi, I want to work with you.!
or
Hey Varun, I am Ravi. Can we hop on a Zoom Session?

No! This is not the way.
Do you think that people would reply to these types of messages? Why People, let's think from your POV, would you reply to these kinds of messages? No, right?

Then, what makes a Person reply?

You need to provide them value, you need to show them that you are a valuable person, you need to show them you're credible.

You need to make them feel that they may get benefitted from you. Speak about how they may get helped due to you. Speak about them.

You can share your Experience, Testimonials in the first message itself. This builds credibility and trust.

To show them that you are credible, you need to show your authority. For building credibility & authority, what you can do is, at the start of the message, you can write about your experience, what you have done. And then speak about how they will be benefited through your experience.

This is a message which I sent for **Podcast Invitation**:

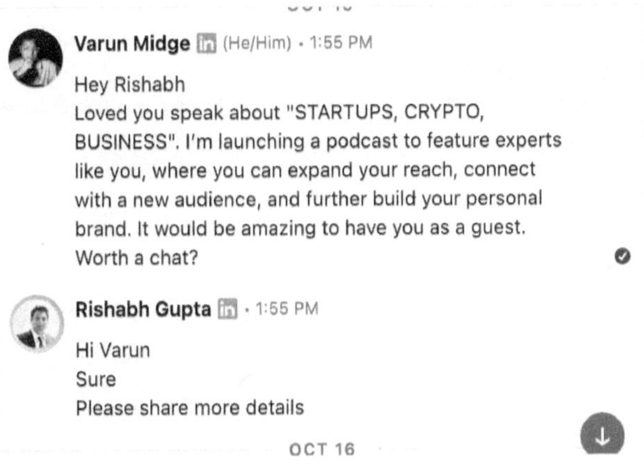

Now, if we decode these messages, what I have done here is: I first wrote about him, praising him. Then I displayed how he would get benefitted through my Podcast.
Simple..!

Another way:

You can also send them a personalized connection request where you can speak something about their recent post. "Why did you like their post?" You can simply give insights about it.

This is a Great way to network with Big People on LinkedIn. In this way, you can become a good friend with them and share benefits rather than being "salesy" or asking for something at the start itself.

For this, I have one trick for you.

You can simply use this chatgpt prompt:
"Hey Chatgpt:
This is the Post of one creator on LinkedIn
Creator's LinkedIn Bio:
Post:
My LinkedIn Bio:
Write a review/insight about this post in 15 words."

This way, chatgpt can help you create a good insight. You can play around with these prompts and make the most out of it.

Cheers..!!

And one more thing, people often accept the connection request and don't reply.

Now, in this case, you have to take follow ups.
For follow ups, you can send them your case studies, your portfolio, your achievements, or a short introduction about yourself.

You can also send them freebies, any free templates or trackers, which might help them. I mean to provide them with some upfront Value which can really help them.

For people outreaching for Jobs, the approach of follow ups might be different. I haven't tried that honestly, so I won't comment on it.

So yeah, that was it in this section, bye. See you in the next section.

LinkedIn Content

Now, I haven't yet cracked the Content Game Myself, hence I don't find myself at the authority of telling you what to do.

But, as per I have studied from various creators like Ishan Sharma, Ankur Warikoo, Vedika Bhaia, I have observed that one thing these guys have in common is consistency, they write a linkedIn post in a specific routine, some post daily, some post thrice a week, but they do it consistently.

And another thing which is common in them is writing, they are the masters of Storytelling.

So, for content, what I would suggest is:
- Be Consistent. Post content consistently. Not daily, but thrice or twice a week.
- Learn how to write content & learn about storytelling.

And that's it.!

Now, let's have a short brief on some Technical Terms.
There are 4 types of LinkedIn Content:
- Written LinkedIn Post
- Image
- Video
- Carousels
- Articles

Written LinkedIn Post & Images:
Even in the Video world, LinkedIn Posts which are so basic, just text, work Great on LinkedIn.

Here, you can share your views on any topic, your personal experiences, your experience of the event you went to, you can post about your job update, you can post about the recruitment drive in your company, the achievements, and the list is endless.

You must have seen many posts on LinkedIn which display a video or a photograph first and then, its explanation is written in the text section.

So, You can do a combination of 1 & 2, 1 & 3, 1 & 4. This works Great..!

You can use various HashTags related to your niche or related to your post. This is the most important thing you need to remember. Hashtags take the post to the target audience and boost the Engagement Rate of the Post.

Start by using hashtags that align with your industry, topic, or audience. For example, if your post is about career growth, hashtags like #CareerDevelopment, #GrowthMindset, or #Leadership are precise and impactful.

The best performing posts I've are people sharing their personal experiences, the struggles they've had. -->

Posts with Pictures or Videos have 98% more engagement than only the written post.

You can create a #Hashtag of your name. People can follow that Hashtag to keep seeing your Posts.

The Power of Personal Stories:
The posts that perform the best are those that share authentic stories. Why? Because they create an emotional connection.
Whether it's about a failure that led to a breakthrough or a milestone that you're celebrating, people appreciate the realness.

Personal stories
- Showcase your journey and make you relatable.
- Invite others to share their own experiences in the comments.
- Encourage meaningful conversations, which LinkedIn's algorithm loves.

The Hook Formula:
Every great post starts with a strong hook—something that stops someone mid-scroll.

Think of your hook as the headline of a newspaper.

Would it make you curious enough to read on?
Examples of effective hooks --->

Examples of effective hooks:
- "I almost gave up, but then this happened…"
- "Here's a mistake I made—and what I learned from it."
- "What if I told you this one skill could transform your career?"
- Billionaire's advice to 20 year olds
- A lot has changed in just a Year
- Watch THIS if you're 20!

Crafting hooks is a skill that improves with practice. You should study high-performing posts on LinkedIn and analyze what makes their hooks compelling. Experiment, tweak, and learn.

Engagement Tips for LinkedIn Posts:
- **Engage back:** If someone comments on your post, reply! Conversations boost visibility and build relationships.
- **Ask questions:** Posts with questions naturally invite comments. For example, "What's your take on this?" or "Have you experienced this too?"
- **Be consistent:** Post regularly, but focus on quality over quantity. Even one valuable post a week can make an impact.

Remember, LinkedIn isn't just about broadcasting; it's about building connections. Every post is an opportunity to share value, foster relationships, and leave a lasting impression.

Here's one of my posts which has done exceptionally well regardless of the number of followers I have.

Varun Midge · You
Helping Businesses & Coaches to Scale by Converting Connections into ...
Book an appointment
6d · 🌐

Pov: You meet Billionaires, founders, 100s of Entrepreneurs

This is was me at TGS Global Summit at Bangalore TiE Bangalore

I met Founders, Investors, Entrepreneurs and the top industry Professionals.

500+ Startups, 500+ Businesses, 1000+ Investors, 5000+ Entrepreneurs and 11000+ Visitors

This #TGS TiE Global Summit 2024 at Bangalore opened my Mind to a lot of new Opportunities, new Ideas, new People, new Perspectives.

It was Incredible and Mind-tuning.

💯It gave me a Brand New Perspective to think.
💯An Innovative perspective to learn.
💯A different way to communicate and connect with People.

I am Grateful that I got the Opportunity to Attend this Summit.
It gave me Learnings for Life long.
Cheers!!!
Thanks TiE Bangalore TiE TiE Mysuru

#TGS2024 #TiE #TiEBangalore #TiEGlobalSummit #entrepreneurship #business #founder #billionaire #learnings #startup #vc #investor

You can check more of my Posts. I keep sharing the Experiences I had, my Learnings, about the Podcast, and various stuff.

LinkedIn Video:

LinkedIn has evolved over the years, and now it's leaning heavily into video content. Recently, LinkedIn introduced a dedicated video section in the app, similar to the Instagram Reels feature.

This move signifies a clear push by LinkedIn to promote video content on the platform, offering a massive opportunity for creators who leverage it effectively.

Think about it—LinkedIn is actively encouraging video posts, which means the algorithm is likely to favor them. Early adopters of this feature can gain significant visibility and engagement.

Whether you're sharing your insights, tips, or experiences, LinkedIn Videos can help you connect with your audience on a more personal level.

Types of Videos You Can Create

Not sure what kind of videos to post? Here are a few ideas:

These things actually can be applied for any platform.

- Insights and Opinions: Share your thoughts on trending topics in your industry. For example, "Why AI is reshaping the marketing landscape."

- Tips and Tutorials: Post short, actionable advice for your audience. "5 tips to improve productivity at work" is a great example.

- Behind-the-Scenes: Show your work process, event preparations, or daily routines. These videos build authenticity.

- Event Highlights: Attended a conference or a seminar? Share snippets and your takeaways.

- Personal Stories: Just like written posts, videos where you share struggles, milestones, or lessons learned perform exceptionally well.

- and you can explore other creative ways

LinkedIn Carousels:

Creators on LinkedIn use different types of Contents to nurture and engage their audience. Carousels are one of them. A LinkedIn Carousel is a post that contains a series of images or slides designed to present information in a structured, step-by-step manner.

They encourage users to scroll through each slide, ensuring they stay engaged with the content from start to finish. This makes Carousels an excellent tool for creators looking to retain their audience's attention and deliver maximum value.

Why Do Carousels Work So Well?

Carousels leverage a simple but powerful concept: curiosity and flow.

- Step-by-Step Narratives: The sequential structure of Carousels builds curiosity, encouraging the audience to keep scrolling to see what comes next.

- Visual Appeal: Eye-catching graphics, bold text, and clean designs make Carousels more engaging than plain text posts.

- Bite-Sized Information: Carousels allow you to break down complex topics into digestible slides, making it easier for your audience to absorb the information.

For example, instead of writing a lengthy post about "10 LinkedIn Tips for Beginners", you can create a 10-slide Carousel with each slide covering one tip.

Ankur Warikoo in · Following
Founder @WebVeda, Content creator @wariCrew, Speaker, Auth...
Visit my website
5d · 🌐

I am conducting my first ever online masterclass on careers - Sunday, January 5, 2025 at 6:30pm. ...more

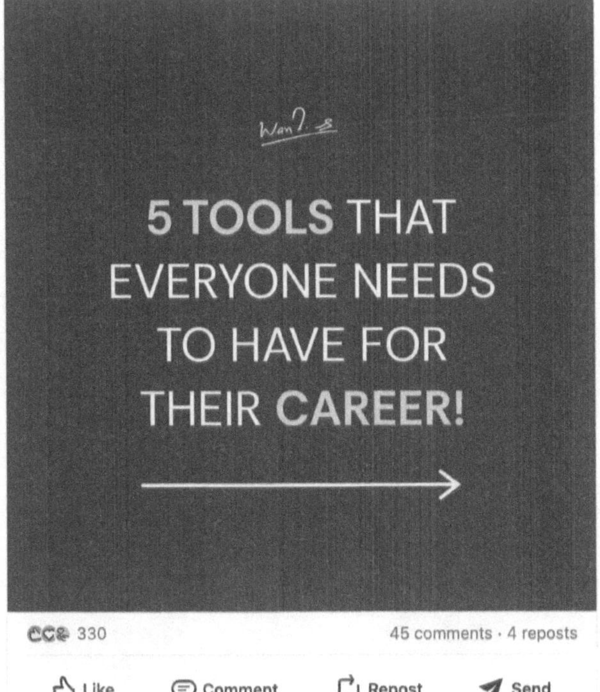

330   45 comments · 4 reposts

👍 Like   💬 Comment   🔁 Repost   ✈ Send

Ankur Warikoo, a creator uses Carousels in a very innovative way to provide value to his audience
This is one of his Posts.

Another Carousel Post by a Creator, **Alex Hormozi**, I have learnt a lot from you about Sales, Online Businesses, etc. You must check out his Content on YouTube. It's a must Learn.

35

LinkedIn Articles:

LinkedIn Articles are similar to Blogs. You can Publish Articles on LinkedIn separately. No domain or website is required for that unlike the Blogs.

The Articles have no Limit to Characters. LinkedIn gives all the text Formatting like Bold Text etc for Articles.

Headlines of the Articles must be catchy like any other Blogs on the Internet.

Why Should You Write Articles on LinkedIn?

- **Showcase Expertise:** You can position yourself as a thought leader by sharing your knowledge.

- **Engage Your Network:** You can provide deeper insights that spark meaningful conversations.

- **Build Credibility:** Your articles can act as a portfolio of your expertise, especially helpful when networking with potential clients or employers.

- **Expand Your Reach:** Articles get distributed not just to your network but to LinkedIn members who might be interested in the topic.

Writing a LinkedIn Post

As we saw in the previous chapter about the Posts. Now, let's see how to write a Post.

A post must have a Hook & a flow like a story. Just like this Post of mine

On 15th Jan 2025, I wrote a Post on LinkedIn about my Experience of Learning from a Billionaire at TGS Summit at Bangalore.

Varun Midge · You

Helping Businesses & Coaches to Scale by Converting Connections into ...

Book an appointment

1w · 🌐

The Billionaire's Advise to 20 Year Olds.....💯

I was at TiE Global Summit at Bangalore in December🔥
& on the 2nd Day, I entered the Place & I saw a lot of People surrounding
someone. It was Dr A Velumani 🔥

The Billionaire Dr A Velumani was just 5 steps away from me!!😵
fyi: He sold his Company Thyrocare Technologies Ltd. for 4546CRORES🔥😵

Someone there, asked him "Sir, what advice would give to 20 Year Old
youngsters?"

What he said wasn't anything extraordinary or different, but Impactful💯.

What he said was just 2 things.
✅ Focus on 1 thing.
✅ Learn as much as you can & Keep Learning.

That's it!

Isn't it TRUE that most successful people on the Internet give similar advice, but
we don't take it? LOL..😅

I am Grateful that I got a chance to Experience his AURA😇

Grateful TiE Bangalore TiE Mysuru
Thanks Dr A Velumani Sir.

P.S. I couldn't click a Photo with him😔

#velumani #thyrocare #TGS2024 #TiE #TiEBangalore #TiEMysuru
#TiEGlobalSummit #entrepreneurship #business #founder #billionaire
#learnings #startup #vc #investor #student #millionaire #money #power
#leadership #TGS #youth

Also, the Billionaire himself liked this Post

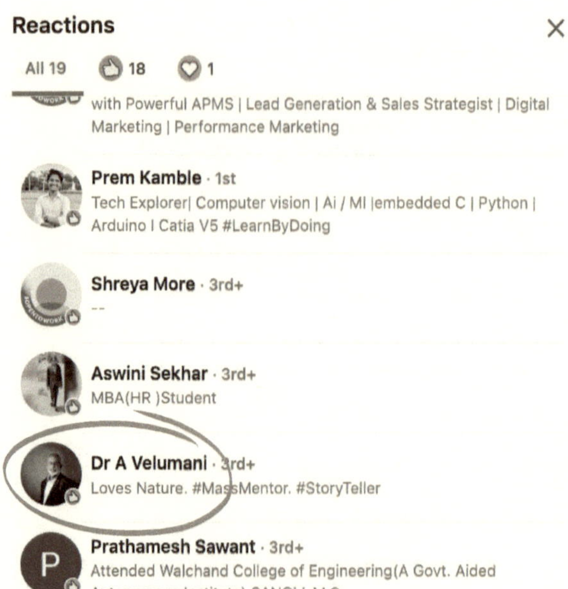

Now, let's decode this Post.

First thing I added is Hook "Billionaire's Advice to 20 Year Olds". After that I started structuring it like a Story and explained the Instance.

I mentioned Dr A Velumani in the Post, and also mentioned his Achievement.

I also mentioned the TiE Bangalore & TiE Mysore Organisations in the Post.

Because I mentioned Dr A Velumani, he was able to reach my Post and engage with it.

I also attached a Video from the Instance.

This is one Learning from this, if you're writing about someone in the Post, always mention them. You can mention them by typing @ following by their name and the drop down appears. You can select and good to go. By just mentioning, LinkedIn sends the notification about this to their followers also.

I also used emojis to describe feelings better.

Some key points --->

Some Key Points:
- Always Mention People if needed
- Always use Bullet Points
- Use Emojis to communicate feelings better
- Give spacing after every 2-3 lines for better looks and readability.

You can also go through Previous Posts on Mine which are better than even this one.

Honestly, this post didn't do well because I posted it at odd time, about 4PM.

Most of my Posts which got good traction were posted in the morning around 11AM

LinkedIn Service Page

There is a Dedicated Page for you to display your Services on LinkedIn likewise the Fiverr, Freelancer.com.

This is how a typical Service Page looks like to a Person.

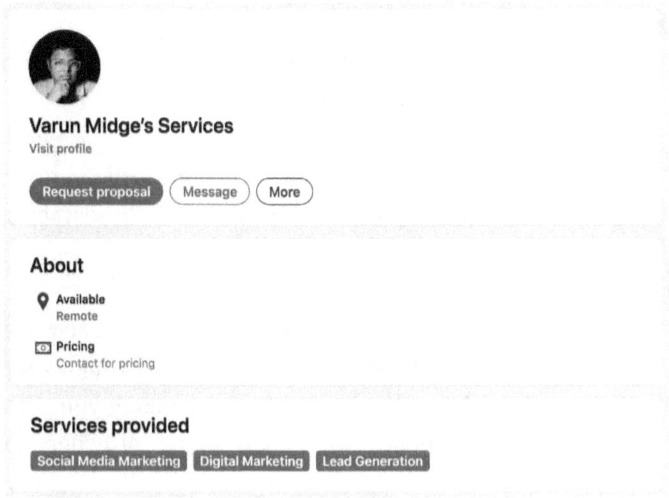

How Does It Work?
Setup:
- You select the services you want to showcase from a predefined list or custom options.
- Choose your availability, work location (remote or local), and other details.
- Publish your page, and it becomes visible to your network and beyond.

Discovery:

- LinkedIn matches your Service Page to potential clients who are looking for similar services.

- This includes people outside your immediate connections, expanding your reach significantly.

Service Requests:

- Once your page is live, you start receiving Service Requests from interested people.

- These requests aren't just limited to your profile visitors; LinkedIn proactively connects you with users searching for your niche.

- The interesting part is that the requests you receive are not always from people who directly apply through your Service Page. LinkedIn's algorithm may match you with people who've applied to similar service providers in your niche.

Why to use the LinkedIn Service Page?

- Visibility to the Right Audience: LinkedIn promotes your Service Page to users actively searching for services in your niche.

- Direct Leads: Unlike traditional posts, the Service Page brings in clients who are ready to collaborate or hire.

- Professional Presentation: It adds credibility to your profile, making you stand out in a competitive market.

- Networking Simplified: It streamlines the process of turning connections into clients.

Example Use Cases:

- A social media marketer can list services like content creation, strategy, and ad management.

- A graphic designer can showcase their skills in logo design, branding, and illustration.

- An AI consultant can offer workshops, implementation strategies, or AI-driven solutions.

LinkedIn Profile Analytics

The LinkedIn Profile Insights section is a powerful tool that provides a comprehensive analysis of your account activity. It allows you to monitor how your profile and posts are performing, offering critical data that can help you optimize your presence on the platform.

1.Post Performance

- You can see how your recent posts performed. Insights into the engagement, likes, comments, and shares each of your posts received.

- You can see which was your best-performing post.

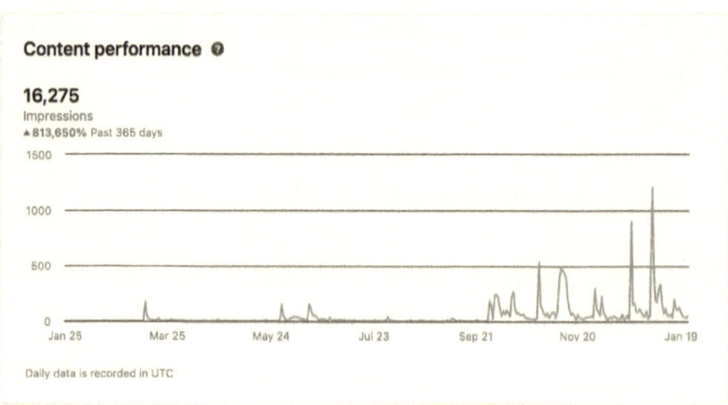

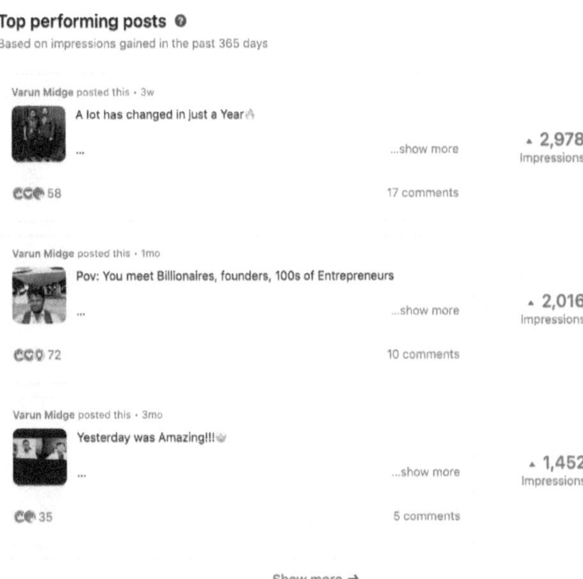

2. Impressions and Reach

- **Post Impressions:** Understand how many people saw your posts. This metric shows the visibility your content achieved.

- **Profile Impressions:** Track the number of views on your profile, indicating how much interest your profile is generating.

3. Audience Insights

Who viewed your profile?

You can see a detailed breakdown of the people visiting your profile, including:
- **Their job roles**
- **The companies they work for**
- **The industries they belong to**
- **Geographic location**

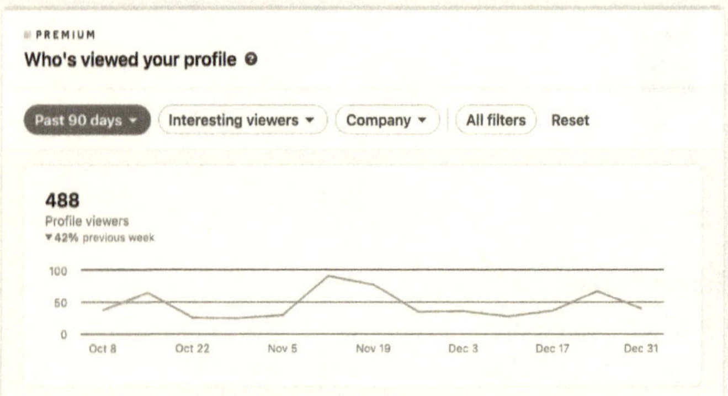

Top demographics ❓

Job titles ▾

Founder · 12.8%

Co-Founder · 5%

Dentist · 4.9%

Chief Executive Officer · 2.7%

Software Engineer · 2.1%

Top demographics ❓

Locations ▾

Pune/Pimpri-Chinchwad Area · 15.5%

Greater Delhi Area · 9%

Mumbai Metropolitan Region · 8.2%

Greater Bengaluru Area · 7.1%

Sangli · 5%

These insights help us to:

Optimize Content Strategy: Use data on post performance to refine the type of content you create. For instance, if your audience engages more with educational posts, focus on creating more of those.

Understand Your Audience: Insights into the industries, companies, and roles of profile visitors help you align your content with their interests.

Expand Your Reach: Knowing who views your profile allows you to reach out and connect with individuals or companies relevant to your goals.

Measure Growth: Regularly tracking impressions and profile views lets you gauge your progress over time.

LinkedIn Jobs

According to me, there are 2 ways to get a Job through LinkedIn:

1. Applying for Job Openings
There are Number of Job Opportunities posted by companies across the globe.

Here's how you can make the most of this feature:
- **Search Smart:** Use filters like location, job type, experience level, and industry to narrow down your search.
- **Set Job Alerts:** Enable job alerts to receive notifications for openings that match your preferences.
- **Optimize Your Application:** Ensure your LinkedIn profile is fully updated, as many companies allow you to apply directly with your profile. A polished, keyword-rich profile increases your chances of standing out.

2. Networking for Referrals
Sometimes, the best way to land a job isn't through the traditional application process but through referrals. Here's how you can leverage LinkedIn to secure them:

- **Build Genuine Connections:** Reach out to people working in companies you're interested in. Start with a personalized message that shows genuine interest in their work.

- **Showcase Your Value:** Share your skills, achievements, and how you can contribute to their organization. Be clear and concise about what you bring to the table.

- **Engage With Their Content:** Like, comment, and share their posts to build rapport before asking for a referral.

- **Be Respectful:** When asking for a referral, ensure your request is polite and considerate. Highlight how your skills align with the company's needs without being overly pushy.

I tried this for one of my friends. What worked was sharing what he learned from his past years of Experience in Previous Companies and how he can add value to another bigger company. If we can sum this up in 300 characters, it's the best way to get a referral.

This was the message I used for him:

"Hii {Name},
I noticed you're a {Position} at {Company}. As a Brand Manager at Amazon, and after serving 40+ Restaurants/Brands at Zomato, Swiggy as a Key Accounts Manager, I figured out what should be the right Content, right Pricing, right Positioning to make a Brand standout in the Market.
I would love to contribute my Learnings at {Company}.
Worth a Convo?"

LinkedIn Ads

LinkedIn Ads are an amazing opportunity for businesses to expand their reach and directly target professionals who matter the most. With over 1 Billion users, LinkedIn allows you to connect with decision-makers, executives, and professionals like no other platform. It's one of the best places to generate leads, increase visibility, and build credibility in your niche.

Types of LinkedIn Ads

LinkedIn offers a variety of ad formats to suit your needs. Here's a quick breakdown:

1. Sponsored Content

These ads appear directly in the LinkedIn feed and look just like regular posts.

- **Single Image Ads:** Perfect for promoting blogs, articles, or any resource with just one strong visual.

- **Video Ads:** Videos are a game-changer on LinkedIn. Use them to tell your brand story, share product details, or provide value.

- **Carousel Ads:** A series of swipeable cards—great for storytelling or showing multiple products/services.

2. Sponsored Messaging

These ads go straight into someone's LinkedIn inbox.

- Message Ads: Deliver a direct, personalized pitch or invite to an event.

- Conversation Ads: These feel like a casual chat, letting users interact and choose their own response path.

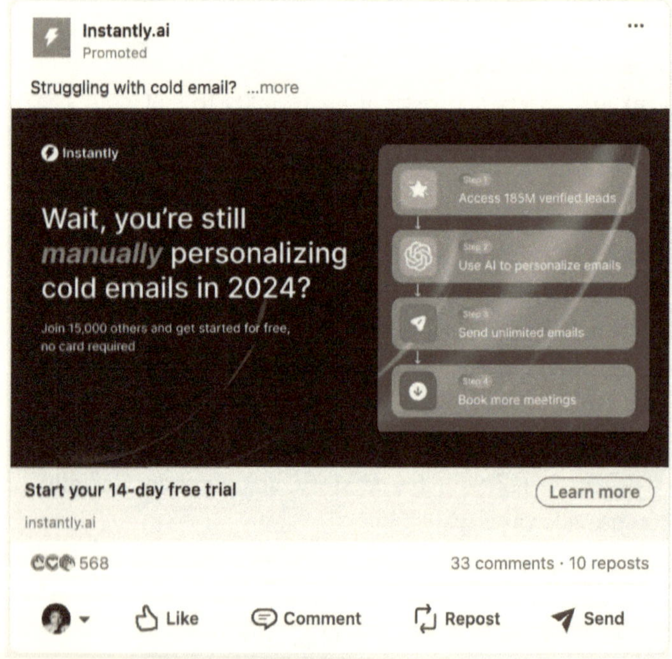

Razorpay
902,261 followers
Promoted

Payroll in a flash? RazorpayX Payroll makes it happen! Calculations, compliance, queries - all in under 5 minutes. Sign up today.

Save 20% This New Year!
921 submits

✎ Sign Up

16

👍 Like   💬 Comment   🔁 Repost   ➤ Send

3. Text Ads

These are simple ads that appear on the sidebar.
They're straightforward, cost-effective, and great for driving traffic to a website or landing page.

4. Dynamic Ads

These personalise content using the viewer's profile details like their name, job title, or company.

- Follower Ads: Encourage users to follow your LinkedIn page.
- Spotlight Ads: Highlight your website or an offer.

5. Lead Gen Forms

These ads make it super easy to collect leads because users don't even have to leave LinkedIn to fill out the form.

Final Thoughts:

LinkedIn Ads might seem expensive compared to other platforms, but the quality of leads and the ability to target professionals make it worth every penny. Whether you're looking to grow your business, generate high-value leads, or build your brand, LinkedIn Ads are a tool you can't ignore. Start small, test everything, and keep improving. Success on LinkedIn Ads is all about consistency and understanding your audience!

Pro Approach

If you want to build Great Connections and Relationships which are beyond just Professionalism. Here are some things you can do:

Comment on the Post:
You can see the recent post of the person and comment on an insight or learning from the Post. Also, you can end the comment with a call to action which can make the Author reply to you.

Share Their Post with Your Insights:
Repost their content with a personalized take on it. Mention what you learned or how it impacted you and tag the author to show appreciation.

Ask Questions in the Comments
Engage by asking thoughtful questions related to the post. This encourages a deeper conversation and positions you as someone genuinely interested.

Messaging them with a Personalisation about Post
You can send them a Connection Request or a Message in which you will write about their recent Post. Maybe your learnings from it, insights, or any questions you have.

Seek Their Advice

People love sharing their expertise. Ask them for advice on a specific topic where you value their knowledge. For example, "I noticed you've been working on [topic]. What would you recommend for someone just starting out in this field?"

Engage Regularly

Don't just comment or message once and disappear. Stay in touch by engaging with their posts consistently or sending occasional messages to check in.

Help Without Expectation

Offer assistance or share resources that might benefit them without expecting anything in return. For instance, if you know someone who could help them with a project, offer to connect them.

By applying these approaches, you'll not only build strong professional relationships but also create meaningful personal connections that can open doors to new opportunities and collaborations. Let me know if you'd like to expand further!

Collaborations

With over 1 billion users, LinkedIn is a goldmine of opportunities for collaboration. Many businesses might differ in what they offer, but they often share the same types of customers. This opens the door for partnerships that can help both parties grow.

Example: **Finding Synergies**

Imagine this scenario:
- You own a **Video Editing Agency**, catering primarily to content creators.
- Your friend owns a **Design Agency**, also serving content creators.

Although your services differ, you're targeting the same audience. This overlap creates a natural synergy where you can:
- **Collaborate on Projects:** Offer bundled services to clients, like video editing and design, to provide a complete solution.
- **Refer Clients:** If your client needs design work, refer them to your friend. Likewise, your friend can send video editing leads your way.
- **Create Joint Offers:** Combine your expertise into a packaged deal that appeals to clients, showcasing your collaborative value.

Now, even if you don't have a friend, you get many people on LinkedIn who are providing complementary services to the same Audience. You can directly get connected with those People and Collaborate with them.

This way, you'll be benefitted by 3 things:
- You get access to the other's Network

- You get access to Directly a Potential Customer, because, if someone is already paying for some sort of service, then can pay you too if your service adds value to them.

- The Prospect trusts you easily, because you're are connected with a person with whom the Prospect is already working

Isn't it Crazy?

DOs on LinkedIn

Whether you are creating content, outreaching for your Business, or outreaching for Jobs. The most important things I want to say are:

Be Consistent:
You cannot send 10 messages today and then be quiet and wait for the reply for the rest of the Month.This won't give you results. You need to send messages everyday.

Make sure you are messaging the People who are Active:
You cannot expect that People will reply if they are not even Active. Hence, make sure you take care of this.

Track the Metrics:
Track the no. of Connection Requests sent, accepted, people replied, etc on everyday. Because, What gets Tracked, Gets Improved. Tracking these metrics will help you improve your strategy. You can figure out what works and what doesn't. I learn this thing from one of my Mentors.

Follow-Ups:
Follow-ups are the crucial part and can be a Game - changer. People often accept the connection request and don't reply. Their chances of replying are more when they are followed up.

DON'Ts on LinkedIn

Don't Spam into People's DMs

Bombarding someone's inbox with generic, irrelevant, or overly promotional messages is the quickest way to lose credibility.

Don't Send Connection Requests Without a Note

You can send a Connection without a Note. But, why not send a Personalized invite, so the person can get a clear idea about the topic.

Argue or Be Negative

Never Argue or make enemies on LinkedIn even if the other person is not behaving rightly. Always avoid the argument.

Connect with Everyone on LinkedIn

Never Connect with Everyone on LinkedIn. Because if you connect with the irrelevant or the People not related to your Niche, then these People won't engage with your Account. This will cause your Post's Engagement.

Building Trust

LinkedIn is a Purely Online Platform. Here, even if you make Great Connections. There is always a Problem of Trust Issues. People won't trust you easily.

So, to make the Trust Process easier, you can implement some things.

Sharing Testimonials
This is the easiest method to build Trust. You can Share the Testimonials of the Previous Clients in the LinkedIn Post or in the Message.

Write a Book or an eBook on your Expertise
Not many People do this, but this is one of the Best Method to gain Credibility and Trust. People think this is not that easy, but Trust Me, it's easier than ever. I have done it and you can do it too. Detailed in the next Topic.

Build a Strong Personal Brand
Trust comes naturally when people feel they know you. Focus on creating a consistent and relatable personal brand on LinkedIn by Posting Relatable Content Consistently.

Writing a Book

Writing a Book and Publishing it has never been easier than it is Today. Today, you can just write an ebook today, and publish it in the next 3 days. It's that easy.

- Publishing a Book makes you an Author.
- It's a powerful addition to your LinkedIn profile and professional portfolio.
- A book can attract clients, collaborators, or employers.

You can start by writing an Focussed eBook on a specific Topic. For Example:

- "10 Strategies to Scale Your Business on LinkedIn."
- "How to Build a Winning Social Media Strategy."

You can take help of AI to write a Book.

Step 1: Plan Your Topics

- List down all the key topics you want to cover in your book.
- Structure them into chapters or sections.

Step 2: Draft Each Chapter

For each topic:

1. Write down what you already know or want to share.
2. Use tools like ChatGPT to refine your ideas:
   a. Feed your notes to ChatGPT and ask it to expand or summarize them in 500 words (or your preferred length).
3. Edit and personalize the content to add your unique voice.

Step 3: Assemble and Polish
- Combine all the chapters into a cohesive book.
- Use free tools like Canva to design an attractive cover and format the interior.

P.S.: This Book is not written by ChatGPT :)

Last Thoughts

Happy to see you here! It's really Great that you came here on the Last Page reading this book! It means you are really serious about your Life.

Now, GO and EXECUTE

Feel free to send a connection request to me on my LinkedIn.

Thanks for reading this Book,
Varun